Dedication
To Rosie, Lily, James and Peter

BARROW
& LOW FURNESS
PAST & PRESENT

Scant attention is paid to the No. 4 double-decker tram by the man with two loose dogs on Duke Street, *c*. 1910. The Raphael Tuck postcard claims that Barrow's docks are 'unrivalled on this coast, save at Birkenhead'.

BARROW
& LOW FURNESS
PAST & PRESENT

JOHN GARBUTT

The
History
Press

First published in 2002 by Sutton Publishing Limited

Reprinted in 2010 by
The History Press
The Mill, Brimscombe Port,
Stroud, Gloucestershire, GL5 2QG
www.thehistorypress.co.uk

British Library Cataloguing in Publication Data
A catalogue record for this book is available from the British Library.

ISBN 978-0-7509-4982-8

Illustrations

Front endpaper: Barrow island and town from Walney, painted by G.H. Andrews in about 1872 and engraved by T.A. Prior.
Back endpaper: The same view as on the front endpaper across Walney channel to Barrow Island and town, 2002. St James's church is right of centre and the Channelside Further Education College to its left.
Half title page: The Duke Street extension to the Strand on a Wrench Series postcard sent in 1906. Also featured are a sailing ship in Buccleuch dock, a steamship in Ramsden dock and tramlines around Schneider Square.
Title page: Lord Frederick Cavendish, brother of the eighth Duke of Devonshire, was moved from the square bearing the family name in about 1970 and now faces the traffic-free front of the town hall.

Typeset in 11/14pt Photina and produced by Sutton Publishing Limited.
Printed and bound in England

Contents

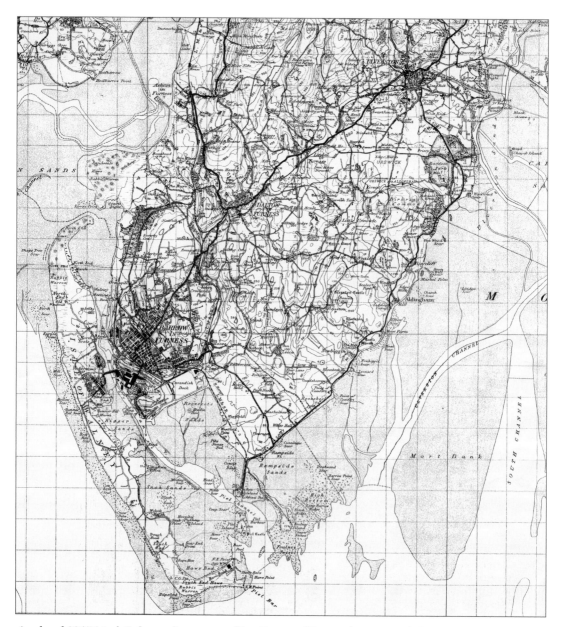

A reduced 1947 1 inch Ordnance Survey map of Low Furness. (*New popular provisional edition*)

Introduction

L ying as it does on the fringe of the Lake District, although in parts heavily industrialised, Barrow-in-Furness derives benefit from clean air from the Irish Sea, countryside recreation areas close at hand, and opportunities for coastal or lake boating, fishing, watersports, etc. Judging from the house prices in Furness, the region is undervalued as a place to live. Road communication is mainly via the A590 into a cul-de-sac some distance from the M6, but this has contributed by protecting much of the rural landscape from the ravages of the developer.

Barrow was included in the Manor of Plain Furness or the Parish of Dalton, which formed the southern tip of the Furness peninsula, stretching north to include Ireleth and Lindal and south to Walney and other smaller islands in the vicinity.

Furness district, the western portion of the old Lancashire North of the Sands and now in South Cumbria, is full of history, in particular industrial history. From 1127 until the Dissolution it was dominated by Furness Abbey, the second richest Cistercian abbey in Britain, much of whose wealth was due to the export of wool. It was thus a prime target

The arms of the County Borough of Barrow-in-Furness granted in 1867 is described as 'Arms: Gules on a bend between in chief a serpent nowed and in base a stag trippant Or an arrow pointing upwards to a bee volant Proper on a chief Argent on waves of the sea a paddlewheel steamship under steam and canvas also Proper. Crest: Out of the battlements of a tower a ram's head Proper armed and collared Or. Motto: *Semper sursum* [always upwards].' (*Boumphrey et al. An armorial for Westmorland and Lonsdale*)

Arms of the Borough of Barrow in Furness.

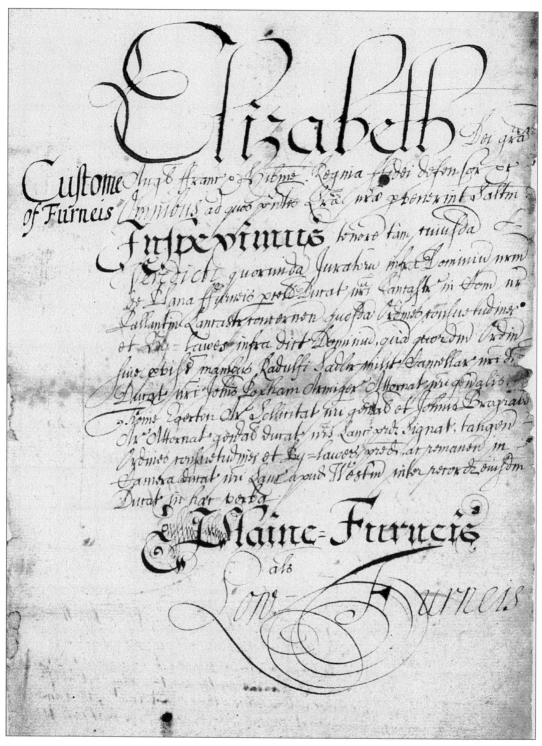

Here is the front page of an early copy of the 1595 Custom of the Manor of Plain Furness, which outlines the local regulations necessary for maintaining order in the area.

for Henry VIII's henchmen at the Dissolution in about 1537. Thereafter Furness was in a very poor state indeed until it was gradually developed, with manufacturing industry and later trade through the port of Ulverston. The port depended upon the Ulverston canal, opened in December 1796, but after a short life this became unusable in the early nineteenth century because of movement of the navigable channel in Morecambe Bay.

Barrow is only briefly described in Baines's Directory of the County Palatine of Lancaster of 1825 under 'Dalton Parish – Villages' as 'a hamlet, 4 miles SSW of Dalton'. Other areas now contained within Barrow – Bigger (now Biggar), Newbarns and North Scales – warranted a longer description. The few prominent citizens of the hamlet mentioned were Joseph Fisher, coal merchant and maltster, Thomas Harrison, victualler, Jacob Parker, coast waiter (customs officer), and John and William Fisher, both yeomen.

In the mid-nineteenth century vast quantities of iron ore were discovered and mined in Furness. This triggered rapid development. A prime mover in the planning of Barrow town, the Furness Railway Company provided rail routes originally built to carry slate and iron ore but which later opened up the district to tourism. Iron was king. Ships were built, factories appeared, the population increased and within twenty to thirty years Barrow's meteoric rise in manufacturing prosperity dominated what is now South Cumbria. So rapid was the development of the town that four churches named after the four gospel saints were opened on the same day – 26 September 1878.

Prominent developers such as H.W. Schneider and in particular Sir James Ramsden and financiers the Dukes of Devonshire and Buccleuch, benefiting from what was virtually a greenfield site, saw to it that the town centre was well provided with wide streets and impressive buildings. Walney and Barrow Islands formed the basis for building extensive sheltered docklands.

Since the late nineteenth century shipbuilding and its ancillary industries have been the major source of employment in the town. Barrow-based companies have been involved at all stages in the development of British naval warfare equipment as well as passenger and cargo ships since mid-Victorian times. From 1904 to the end of the Second World War the main output from the shipyards was conventional submarines built by Vickers, who later joined with the Armstrong Whitworths of Newcastle-upon-Tyne to form Vickers Armstrong Ltd. Later, in 1960, came the Royal Navy's first nuclear submarine, Dreadnought. The shipyard is now used by BAE Systems.

Throughout the last century purchasers of craft have been as diverse as the Royal Navy, the Imperial Japanese and South American navies, Shell, Esso and BP for tankers and the Isle of Man Steam Packet Company and Furness Railway Company for passenger ships. Barrow shipbuilding, like most industries, has had its good and bad years through the late nineteenth and twentieth centuries. The two wars meant that production was in full swing, but also made the shipyard a target for enemy bombers. Fashions in sea transport and world economies have affected its prosperity but throughout it was and is supported by its proud tradition of engineering excellence.

The rest of Low Furness, although occupying only a minor portion of this book, has much to offer in its long history. Dalton, which is close to Furness Abbey, was the 'ancient capital of Furness' during the active time of the abbey.

Ulverston was developed later, although its parish church reputedly had been founded in 1111, sixteen years before the foundation of the abbey. During its development the town obtained power for corn, paper and cotton mills, a foundry and tanneries, and fed the mile-long canal from a network of streams, most of which ran into Carter Pool and out to sea. In 1874 a large iron works, with four, then later six blast furnaces, was constructed close to the canal and shoreline by Harrison, Ainslie & Company. This was replaced in the 1950s by Glaxo's

The Manor of Plain Furness distinguished as it ought to be from the Lordship or Liberty of Plain Furness properly consists of Nothing more than Certain Customary Rents & other Rents called Grunhew Rents, the former payable by equal portions att Whitsuntide & Martinmas the latter att Whitsuntide only & is divided into several Bailywicks viz. Marton & Sealsbank Lindall Ireleth with Marsh Grange. Rampside New Towne Roose & Roose coat Hawk. Newton with Bellincoat Walney Island subdivided into Northscale North End Biggar & South End Old Barrow Island Barrowhead with Hindpool Hawcoat & Newbarnes. Salthouse Cocken Bolton (called in the Rental Lowerbarrow & Shortfield & free Rents very falsely) Bardesay (put under the same head of Lowerbarrow & Shortfield & also falsely deemed a free Rent by the Rental) Angerton Moss & Egton & Newland (for which last there being a particular Court kept is called a Manor & I have made a distinct Rental for that Bailywick) the free Rents & free farm Rents inserted herein properly belonging to the Lordship or Liberty of Furness, & ought to be put thereto, And the fines upon Alienations by discent or purchase of these Customary Lands, which by custom are ascertained att two Years reserved Rent, And the fines Issue. & Americaments of two Court Barons held for the said Manor att Dalton every Year the one upon the 13th. of Octr. when the Court Leet & Court Baron for the Liberty is held, the other in the Month of May or June

This Manor did also belong to the Abby of Furness & came into the Hands of the Crown by the Surrender of the Abbot of this with their other possessions to K. Henry the 8th & remained in the Crown till Granted by K. Charles the Second in 1662. to the Duke of Albemarle.

But during the time it remained in the Crown several parts were parted away by Grants of the Crown of the Demesne Lands & of several parts of the Customary Lands in fee farm reserving small Rents & also by Grants of several of those fee farm Rents afterwards, to instance the Chief of which is the Grant of the Demesnes in fee farm in ye 5th. of K. James the first reserving 76:13:2. to Robert Earl of Salisbury, & ye Grant of the Rent itself to Wm. Earl of Salisbury in ye 12th. Year of the same king, which demesnes now belong to Sr. Tho. Lowther Baronet, whose father married the heiress of the Prestons, who purchased them from the Salisbury Family, so that what is here called the free farm Rents are the Rents reserved upon such Grants, & which were not granted away till the Grant to the Duke of Albemarle, & the

This rental book for the manor of Plain Furness of 1738 has the bailiwicks of Old Barrow Island and Barrowhead with Hindpool featured as only part of the list of districts we would include in the Barrow-in-Furness we know today. In a neat hand it continues by outlining the early history of the local landowners.

pharmaceuticals factory producing antibiotics and other drugs, which is still in existence and developing today.

Between Barrow, Dalton and Ulverston lie a number of villages, with many areas untouched by recent history. Iron mining has scarred the landscape in places leaving its characteristic red soil. Stone from the limestone deposits across the middle of Furness appears in Ulverston and district buildings and country walls, while an area of sandstone at Hawcoat provided red stone for many Barrow constructions.

Among the prominent sons of Furness have been George Romney (1734–1802), the artist, of Dalton, and Sir John Barrow (1763–1848), Secretary of the Admiralty and co-founder of the Royal Geographical Society, Stan Laurel (1890–1965), the comedian, and Lord Justice Norman Birkett (1883–1962), who was one of the two British judges at the post-Second World War Nuremburg trial, and later Lord Justice of Appeal, all of Ulverston.

The theme of this book is of course changes in the Barrow area seen through pairs of early and late photographs or sequences of views through the twentieth century. The district has seen so many alterations in function, fashion, security and prosperity that we can only scratch the surface. Wherever possible the same vantage points have been used for each pair.

A group of pottery pieces, popular in the late nineteenth and early twentieth centuries, shows some of the heraldic symbols adopted by local towns and establishments in the Low Furness area. The popular belief is that all such pieces were sold only in the named resort.

Central Barrow

This early photograph, taken by Horner of Settle probably in about 1860, has two spectators on an undeveloped Barrow Isle in the foreground, with St George's church prominent in the town and sailing ships berthed in what became Devonshire and Buccleuch docks.

The Coliseum cinema at the corner of Abbey Road and Rawlinson Street, which showed continuous films from 6.30 to 10.30 p.m.

The Coliseum site now serves as a grass verge and car park for local shops.

On the opposite corner its successor, first named the Ritz and then the Apollo, is itself confronted by a 'conserve or demolish' debate. It has been superseded by the Apollo cinema, Hollywood Park, Hindpool Road.

King's Hall at the corner of Hartington and Nelson Streets, seen on this Frith's postcard, once attracted such international singers and instrumentalists as John Heddle Nash, Solomon, and Rawicz and Landauer. Barrow Grammar School speech day ceremonies were held there and a Methodist mission was situated behind the hall. (*Delya Slater*)

The hall, having lost its crown and with a changed front entrance, now houses the Furness Gymnastics Club. Trees are now well established along Hartington Street.

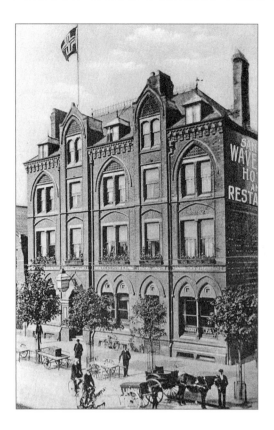

Mrs J.B. Sansom's Waverley hotel and restaurant was on Abbey Road, as seen here with horse-drawn carriage and porters with carts waiting for guests, *c.* 1910. (*Delya Slater*)

It was bombed during the Second World War and has been replaced by the well-cared-for Coronation Gardens here overlooked by the magistrates' court.

This Raphael Tuck postcard of Abbey Road with double-decker tram and unhurried pedestrians in 1906 quotes: 'Handsome buildings are on each side of the way, and tastes social and ecclesiastical are satisfied, or ought to be, by five churches, two clubs and a working men's institute.'

From a nearby viewpoint, we see in 2002 the working men's club, Ramsden Hall, and the technical college now refurbished, joined by the Bar Continental, two generations of telephone kiosks, busy car lanes and pedestrians protected by a traffic island and a zebra crossing.

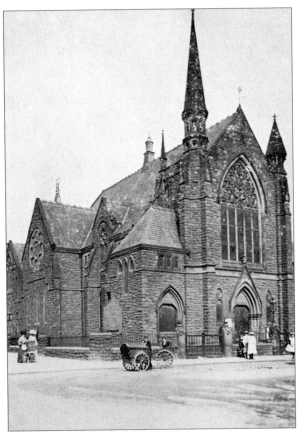

Christ church, here on a postcard with a Davis photograph, *c.* 1910, at the corner of Abbey Road and Dalkeith Street, was bombed during the Second World War. (*Delya Slater*)

Part of the church buildings are still evident above the DS Fitness Centre, more so at the rear, but the corner site is now occupied by Hewden's tool and equipment hire shop.

This high viewpoint picture across Ramsden Square in 1895 shows, left to right, the flax and jute works, the Foresters' Hall at the base of the huge jute works chimney and the Haematite Iron and Steel works chimneys on the horizon with consequent atmospheric pollution. (*Delya Slater*)

The same scene in 2002, taken from the NatWest building through birdproof netting, shows the enlarged roundabout, the chimneys and pollution absent. The bus terminus on the left is backed by shops in Hindpool Park and the Craven Park rugby football stadium. The Foresters' building still stands and a corner of the library is seen on the extreme right.

A Photochromic Company postcard of around 1905, showing Duke Street, has the town hall prominent with No. 109 on the corner of Parade Street advertising a Fry's product. It was occupied by the United Counties bank from around 1913, then Barclay's bank from 1917.

A wider view from Ramsden Square in 2002 has No. 109 with changed windows and redecoration becoming the Old Bank public house. Most of the structures of the other buildings on the right have changed little. The photographer standing on a traffic island in Ramsden Square felt more vulnerable than the children appeared to be in the picture above.

This scene at Schneider Square, *c.* 1905, with single-decker No. 9 tram on its way to Roose leaving and double-decker No. 4 approaching the statue which faces Michaelson Road, shows the town hall under repair with scaffolding. (*Delya Slater*)

In 2002 we see the same scene with Schneider's statue turned to face Duke Street and surrounded by new plainer railings and an attractive roundabout.

A Stengel postcard has Schneider Square looking towards the extension of Duke Street, *c*. 1905, showing working men and children posed for the photograph. Dr Carmichael's surgery, the Albion hotel and the old general post office face the statue.

In 2002, with the three buildings remaining, we see much naval construction activity behind in Buccleuch dock.

In about 1908, on this Valentine's postcard, Lord Frederick Cavendish's statue dominates the square bearing his name. No. 1 double-decker tram and a horse-drawn carriage compete for passengers. The tramway office with its waiting room stands on the right with J. Jackson & Son tailors next to Barrat's Phonographics. Behind was the Salvation Army citadel. To the right of centre was Pass & Co., wholesale merchants, later selling anything 'From a Pin to a Piano'.

In 2002 Cavendish Square is now a pedestrian precinct and the statue of Sir Frederick Cavendish has been removed to the other side of the town hall. The one-time Pass's Emporium and the citadel, then the Palace of Varieties which became the Palace cinema, have been replaced by Yates's Wine Lodge and Wilkinson's hardware store.

The open market in Market Street next to the town hall was a busy place at the turn of the century with stalls, sideshows and a fairground.

Now, in 2002, Market Street has become part of a Duke Street diversion round the town hall with the police station supervising the many law-abiding motorists.

Dalton Road, here relatively quiet, on a Valentine's postcard, *c.* 1910. At No. 151 is A. Whitehouse, the boot dealer. Opposite, from the right, are Miss Turvey, milliner, M.E. Stead, butcher, Gilbert & Sons, jewellers and watchmakers to the Admiralty, G. Blair, tobacconist and T.C. Palmer, prominently advertised as Barrow's smart tailor.

Today, in 2002, we see on the left there is still a shoe shop – Barratts. Most of the buildings are significantly modernised and the road is now pedestrianised so that mysterious dark-clad strangers on bicycles are prohibited.

North Lonsdale hospital was impressive as seen here early last century. It was constructed in about 1870, at the time when Barrow was developing rapidly, caring for industrial accidents, epidemics, and so on.

The much-needed Furness General hospital was first opened to patients, to replace North Lonsdale and other local hospitals, in October 1984 on an out-of-town site with plenty of space for development. It was officially opened by Her Majesty the Queen in May 1985.

St George's Church & Outer Barrow

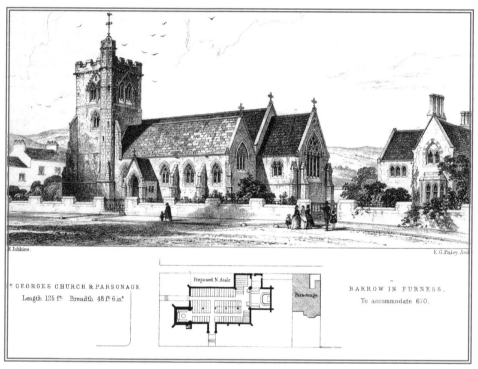

ˣ GEORGES CHURCH & PARSONAGE
Length 125 fᵗ Breadth 48 fᵗ 6 inˢ

Proposed N. Aisle

Parsonage

BARROW IN FURNESS.
To accommodate 670.

R.Jobbins.

E.G.Paley. Arcʰ

St George's, the oldest church in Barrow, with its parsonage. Designed by E.G. Paley, the church was built in about 1860. Both still stand on a prominent site with a good view of much of the area.

The south-west face of St George's church alongside North Lonsdale hospital, *c.* 1905.

In 2002 we have the same aspect of St George's church, but with the hospital site cleared.

A view of Barrow from the top of St George's church tower looking down Church Street towards the town hall, *c.* 1910. On Albert Street (the corner is right of centre) were Her Majesty's theatre and Thomson and Sons' mineral water manufacturers.

Above & below: Two 2002 scenes looking in the same direction as the previous one start a full circle series of fourteen views from the top of St George's church tower. We see the Strand and Devonshire Dock Hall on the left; several houses have been removed on the left of Church Street and the back of Albert Street. On the right centre of the lower picture the old hospital nurses' home is now Rustlings Court flats.

Three scenes over Barrow show the cleared North Lonsdale hospital site in the foreground, the back of the nursing homes Risedale at St George's (with external staircase) and Risedale at Lonsdale (with gable end beyond), and School Street with the older hospital 'supported by voluntary contributions' (now terraced houses) stretching towards Salthouse Road.

Traffic along Salthouse
Road passes the ends
of School Street and
Rawlinson Street, 2002.

The large patch of clear
ground borders Cavendish
dock, with Roosecote power
station left of centre and the
British Gas onshore terminal
visible on the right horizon.

On St George's Square,
opposite the church from
which the panorama was
taken, were the Furness
Railway Company general
offices. This picture was
taken in 1907.

More of Cavendish dock in 2002 with part of Ramsden dock on the extreme right.

The continuation of the Strand, Cavendish Dock Road, with a line of parked cars, is alongside Buccleuch dock, which merges into Ramsden dock.

Three 2002 photographs show most of Buccleuch dock with twin assault ships *Albion* and *Bulwark* berthed and being fitted. Between the two ships and below on the Strand is the railwaymen's club.

Continuing along the Strand we see the corner of St George's Square with the building which was occupied by the Lancaster Banking Company, then the Manchester and Liverpool District Banking Company and later the North Lonsdale Hospital Post Graduate Centre. Above is Buccleuch dock in 2002 with the *Bulwark* berthed under a shipyard crane.

More of the Strand in 2002 with the P&O ship European Mariner in front of Michaelson Road bridge and, beyond, BAE Systems Devonshire Dock Hall. This view links up with the first of the panorama photographs.

Constructed of red sandstone the tower was fitted with a roof during the Second World War and was used as an observation post by the Civil Defence, as seen here in the late 1950s with two horses and cart from Jack Bircher's farm. On a good day, from the top, Scotland, North Wales, the Isle of Man and even Ireland were visible. It was later said to be unsafe, and was demolished and used as hardcore under the roads of the Ormsgill estate. (*Ruth and Thomas Bircher*)

Hawcoat tower, *c.* 1913. It is said to have been a watchtower built by a shipowner to view his fleet. (*Delya Slater*)

The tower site in 2002 occupied by grass and a barbed-wire fence.

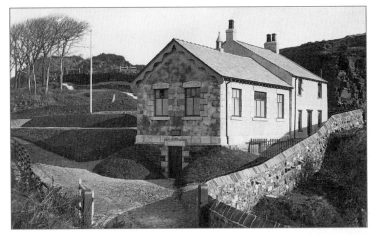

An early Sankey postcard shows the artist George Romney's boyhood home from 1742–55, which was restored by the Furness Railway Company in 1909. A museum was built on the site of the old workshop. The entrance fee was 1*d*. It backed on to the brink of a deep sandstone pit.

A copy of Romney's self-portrait in soft pastel. The original can be seen in the National Portrait Gallery.

Romney Cottage, occupied now but still a tourist attraction, is seen on the left in 2002, with garage attached.

Crowds always lined the streets to watch carnivals in aid of local charities. Here we see an Athersmith's open lorry featuring popular music at the corner of Abbey Road and Ainslie Street in the 1940s. Ashcroft's and Jones & Sons vehicles were acting as observation posts. (*Delya Slater*)

On the same corner in 2002 is the Norwood Medical Centre and still a chemist on the left, with flats on the right which have replaced the Emmanuel Congregational church.

The Lakeland Dyers and Cleaners float at the Ainslie Street corner. This picture shows a similar parade to the one on the previous page. (*Delya Slater*)

In contrast, in 1988, near the Ramsden Square roundabout, the 'Barracudas' provided a mobile model submarine. It must have been a tiring walk for the occupants on a hot day.

Barrow Island & Walney

Photographed probably in about 1960, Walney Island lighthouse is little changed today, still in smart white paint. It is the last surviving manned lighthouse in the United Kingdom. The original was built in 1790 costing £1,100, but burnt down and was rebuilt in 1803. The replacement survives in 2002 under the Lancaster Ports Commissioners of Glasson Dock. A Crosfield of Arnside prawner can be seen on the right.

Looking back from Barrow Island over Michaelson Road high level bridge, *c.* 1910. Caught by the Barrow photographer, W. Cookson, the smartly dressed crowds, followed by a double-decker tram, are probably on their way to a launch. VIPs took coaches guarded by the local constabulary. (*Delya Slater*).

The same scene on a quiet day in 2002. The old post office on the right of centre and the town hall on the left still stand but most of the other buildings have been replaced.

Posted in June 1909, this postcard shows crowds of workers emerging from the shipyard entrance on Michaelson Road. Warehouses adjacent to Devonshire dock are visible on the right. (*Delya Slater*)

The same shipyard entrance in 2002, almost totally rebuilt, is still in the traditional red sandstone. The site is occupied by BAE Systems.

Photographed in about 1908, Egerton Buildings on Barrow Island conveniently housed many shipyard workers. (*Delya Slater*)

Egerton Court off Ramsden Dock Road, 2002. The windows and chimneys have been modified and the interiors reconstructed.

This view card was posted a month after the Walney bridge was opened on 30 July 1908, attended by crowds and much ceremony. The bridge cost £175,000 and at first charged a toll. At a meeting held by the Vickerstown people's committee on 26 June 1908, the subject for discussion was 'the inhabitants of Vickerstown and Barrow are in danger of having the consummation of their hopes for improved access to and from the Island destroyed by reason of the action of some of the owners of pleasure sailing boats in Walney Channel, who wish the bascules of the bridge raised for them each time they wish to pass up and down the Channel'. (*Delya Slater*)

Walney bridge as it is in 2002 with Devonshire Dock Hall behind left of centre and the engine-testing exhaust chimney in the centre.

An excellent view by Sankey of Walney Bridge, the steam ferry and two rowboat ferries on a card posted in August 1927. The steam ferry seems to be neglected with a rowboat stern heavy and overloaded. (*Delya Slater*)

The Ferry hotel watches over the launching site of the old steam ferry in 2002.

Looking across part of Walney channel, with the promenade on the left. North Scale dates back at least to the thirteenth century when it was owned by Furness abbey.

Seen in 2002, North Scale has changed little except to support numerous small craft.

External steps to the first floor are typical of some of the older buildings. Those seen here are on the 'Old Cobbler's Shop' in North Scale early last century. (*Delya Slater*)

All that remains of the cobbler's shop in 2002, showing the primitive wall construction.

A busy Walney channel, *c.* 1920, flanked by the Vickerstown Methodist church and tower on the left and Barrow Haematite Iron and Steel works' chimneys and furnaces on the right. The postcard was published by Sankey.

A similar view of Walney channel in 2002 has the old Methodist church with the top of its tower absent. Black Combe is in the background and the iron and steel works, replaced by modern factories, are fronted by the new Red Man Way – a path running parallel to Walney channel.

A Sankey postcard of Beach Crescent on Walney Island shows these well-constructed houses near Biggar Bank in about 1926. (*Delya Slater*)

The street has changed little, apart from redecoration, in 2002. In the centre is the BAE Systems engine testing exhaust chimney. Local transport has become mechanised.

Here, on a Wrench series postcard sent as a Christmas card in 1903, is Mikasa Street off Ocean Road soon after it was built as part of the celebrated Marine Garden City in Vickerstown. (*Delya Slater*)

By 2002 the Mikasa Street sash windows and designer fences and gates have been replaced by ones of more individualistic design.

Biggar Bank on a busy day, *c.* 1910. It was a popular playground for the inhabitants of Barrow.

A similar view of Biggar Bank in 2002 is almost deserted. It is a favourite place to take the dog for a walk. The wind is bracing. Apart from losing a few chimneys, the houses on the left have changed little, but the buildings in the distance including the pavilion have disappeared.

The Queen's Arms at Biggar village, with chickens, as seen on a Sankey postcard early last century, was once a farmhouse and may be the oldest inn in Furness. Bigger, as the name was spelled in Edward Baines's directory of 1825, was in the township of Hawcoat. Walney Island has long been the subject of erosion by the sea. A decree issued in Hilary term 1565, naming the island 'Wowney', complains that land in North Scale Southend and Northend and Bigger 'is utterly decayed and lost' being 'overflowed by the sea'.

The Queen's Arms in 2002 retains its old-world charm, advertising 'King size meals at the Queens'. Distances seem much further than anticipated on the island, which has excellent nature reserves at the north and south ends.

The open-air swimming pool on Biggar Bank, Walney, with its numerous changing rooms and high diving platforms, *c.* 1930.

Looking at the same site in 2002 it is difficult to believe that on Biggar Bank there was once a boating pool behind the photographer, and in front a sandpit for children and the large swimming pool pictured above.

Industry & Transport

An impressive combination of industry and transport shows the first unit of the assault ship *Bulwark* being moved recently along Bridge Road from the Devonshire Dock Hall to its berth. (*BAE Systems*)

A disastrous fire took place in 1906 at Joseph Waddington's foundry in Hindpool Road. The foundry, established in 1860, carried out 'all kinds of smith work, steam winches, marine repairs, graving dock repairs, pump, hydraulic and general castings and brass castings of every description'. Caird's foundry was also on Hindpool Road opposite the custom house and nearer to the iron and steel works. (*Delya Slater*)

Waddington's factory site, formerly used by Docker's wholesale fruit and vegetable store, is occupied in 2002 by Mark Turner's fresh fruit and vegetables, Dandy's furniture store and the Regal MOT garage.

The Barrow steam corn mill was situated, as here in 1910, between the Hindpool Road gas works and Devonshire dockside warehouses. Started in 1871 and once occupied by Walmsley and Smith, the factory was abandoned in the late 1960s. The Michaelson Road high level bridge can be seen on the bottom right of the picture. (*Delya Slater*)

The corn mill was demolished and the extensive open site is now, in 2002, used by CPL Distribution, 'Britain's leading coal merchants'. Part of the high level bridge can be seen in front of the BAE Systems dockside crane.

As seen here in 1895 the flax and jute mills were impressive, built of red sandstone. Founded by James Ramsden in 1870, they were intended to employ mainly female labour in the factory, as well as many women and children in their homes. In all, the works covered a roughly square area stretching as far as Duke Street. See *Barnes, Barrow and District* (1951).

The corner of the flax and jute works site at the junction of Abbey Road and Hindpool Road is occupied in 2002 by the John Whinnerah Institute.

An opportune photograph looking along Dundonald Street, by Sankey, catches the fall of the jute works chimney on 12 February 1930. The works had suffered fires in 1879 and 1892. (*Delya Slater*)

Looking down Dundonald Street, 2002. St Mary's presbytery and school are on the right. Devonshire Dock Hall is in the centre and the roof and chimneys of the Foresters' building are still visible, to the left of centre.

The iron works, here on a Valentine's Series postcard posted in 1915, which generated the huge neighbouring slag banks, displays its collection of chimneys and blast furnaces. It was close to Walney channel, and with the Bessemer steel works it both produced large quantities of railtrack and used an extensive rail network.

All that remains in 2002 of the iron and steel works, apart from part of the slag heaps, is this sandstone wall and gate with a commemorative plaque on Walney Road and a pond now surrounded by vegetation.

The *Barrow and District Year Book* for 1918 shows the new gasworks at Salthouse, opened the year before, with a single full gasometer. Roose hospital, now demolished and replaced by a housing estate, can be seen in the centre background.

In vast contrast is an aerial view of the South Morecambe and North Morecambe gas terminals between Rampside Road and Roosecote Sands, seen in 2002. The spacious open pipework layout seems almost text-book diagrammatic in nature. Care has been taken to make the sites environmentally inconspicuous from the land side. The enterprise is continuing to expand. (*Picture courtesy of British Gas Hydrocarbon Resources Ltd*)

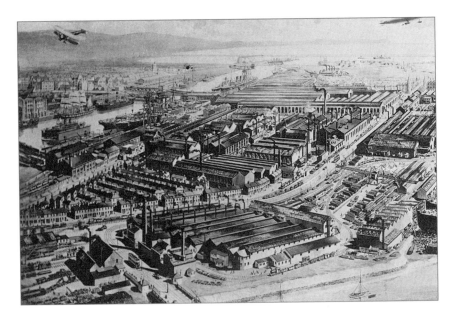

In the age of airships and early biplanes a Sankey aerial photograph postcard shows the extent of Vickers shipbuilding works on Barrow Island in the early twentieth century. A portion of Barrow town is seen behind Devonshire, Buccleuch and Ramsden docks leading to the Walney channel.

An aerial view of the BAE Systems shipyard from the south in the summer of 2000 sees Walney bridge on the left, pointing at Devonshire dock. Black Combe overlooks in the background. Numerous new buildings are evident, and two ships under construction. Left of centre is the engine testing house with its exhaust chimney. Egerton Court is in the right bottom corner. (*BAE Systems Marine Ltd*)

Macro engineering in progress around 1910. On a Sankey postcard we have Vickers Naval Construction Works, showing turbines being erected in pits. The men are dwarfed by the huge components being assembled.

In the Devonshire Dock Hall with VSEL in control, again the scale of construction seems huge in the submarine assembly area. On completion, the vessels are launched directly into Devonshire dock. (*BAE Systems Marine Ltd*)

The number of men featured here in waistcoats and shirtsleeves in the Vickers Maxim works steel foundry, *c*. 1910, points to more hot manual work being necessary than would be the case today.

Again in the Devonshire Dock Hall, now the ultra-modern centre of BAE Systems vessel assembly operations, the work is impressive in scale. The men and fork lift trucks appear like Dinky toys compared with the vessels under construction. (*BAE Systems Marine Ltd*)

On a Sankey postcard sent on 10 March 1913 cantilever cranes overlook intricate scaffolding and launch sites at the Vickers naval construction works. (*Delya Slater*)

The Royal Navy assault vessel L15 *Bulwark* launched stern first down a slipway into Walney channel, 15 November 2001. The guide ropes appear too slender to have had any effect on the movement of the vessel. (*BAE Systems Marine Ltd*)

The P&O Steam Navigation Company liner *Strathmore* was launched in April 1935. It sported a single yellow funnel when commissioned for the England to Australia run, but functioned as a troopship for the Royal Navy during the Second World War.

Again we see the Royal Navy assault ship L15 *Bulwark*, as launched by BAE Systems in 2001. Watched by Tug A222 *Nimble*, it needed drag chains to slow its progress into Walney channel. (*BAE Systems Marine Ltd*)

A Sankey postcard, posted in 1923, that is full of interest. It is taken from Walney looking towards Barrow Island, and features horse-drawn carriages attending the local double-decker tram. Many of the children wear Eton collars and the black horse has a well-earned refreshment of oats in its nose bag.

A contrast in transport is seen in 2002 with cars lined up in the Tesco car park. Looking towards Hindpool Road, we have in the foreground what was the site of the old Jute rail sidings with part of the Jute Works beyond – now Hindpool Park.

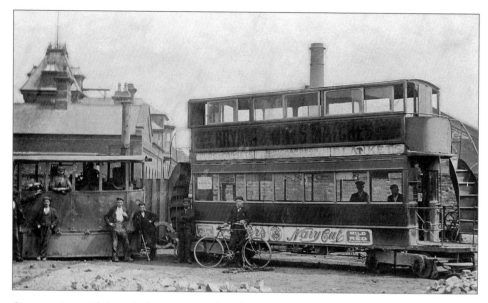

Steam engines with tram trailers were introduced into Barrow in 1885. This example with enclosed upper deck and external staircase advertises Bryant and May's matches, Player's mild and medium Navy Cut tobaccos and Keatings lozenges. There is also a plea to 'Support Home Industries', and a Barrow Tramways public notice: 'No cars will run Saturday . . .'. B. Richardson of Duke Street sold furs, corsets and blankets.

In total contrast in April 2002 we have this Stagecoach local service bus with drivers changing at the terminus off Ramsden Square. The Foresters' building is seen behind with broken attic windows.

This copy of *Railway Economy: a treatise on the new art of transport*, by Dionysius Lardner, DCL &c was owned by James, later Sir James Ramsden, principal founder of Barrow-in-Furness. It was published in 1850 and possibly inspired Ramsden when he first became associated with the Furness Railway Company.

RAILWAY ECONOMY:

A TREATISE ON THE

NEW ART OF TRANSPORT,

ITS

MANAGEMENT, PROSPECTS, AND RELATIONS,
COMMERCIAL, FINANCIAL, AND SOCIAL.

WITH AN EXPOSITION OF

THE PRACTICAL RESULTS OF THE RAILWAYS IN OPERATION IN
THE UNITED KINGDOM, ON THE CONTINENT,
AND IN AMERICA.

BY DIONYSIUS LARDNER, D.C.L. &c.

" There be three things which make a nation great and prosperous ; a fertile soil, busy workshops, and easy conveyance of men and things from one place to another." — BACON.

" Let us travel over all the countries of the earth, and wherever we shall find no facility of passing from a city to a town, or from a village to a hamlet, there we may pronounce the people to be barbarians." — RAYNAL.

LONDON:
TAYLOR, WALTON, AND MABERLY,
UPPER GOWER STREET, AND IVY LANE, PATERNOSTER ROW.
1850.

Stand No. 829 at the Franco-British Exhibition in London was occupied by the Furness Railway Company in 1908 and featured the English Lakeland. The FR sold out to LMS in 1923. (*Delya Slater*)

White-collar workers stream out of the Furness Railway Company general offices and works at the corner of the Strand and Salthouse Road, *c.* 1900.

In 2002 part of the offices are now occupied by Auto Image car sales but the original works has almost completely disappeared. The fine wall along Salthouse Road remains, and even the iron railings have survived, not having been taken for scrap in the war effort.

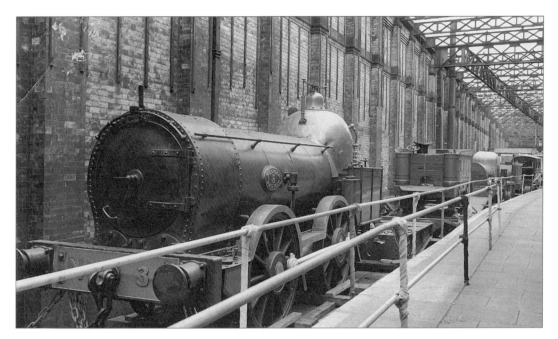

The handsome Furness Railway No. 3 engine is seen without its funnel at the 1951 Festival of Britain exhibition of historic rolling stock in Liverpool Exchange station. Known as Bury's 'Old Copper Nob' it was a passenger engine built in 1846. Its tender held 1,000 gallons, the heating surface of tubes and firebox totalled 854 sq ft and the total weight of the engine and tender was 32 tons 8 cwt.

The engine was for many years a familiar landmark in a glass case outside Barrow railway station. Here, with its funnel replaced, it appeared in 1996 at Haverthwaite at the 150th anniversary of the founding of the Furness Railway Company.

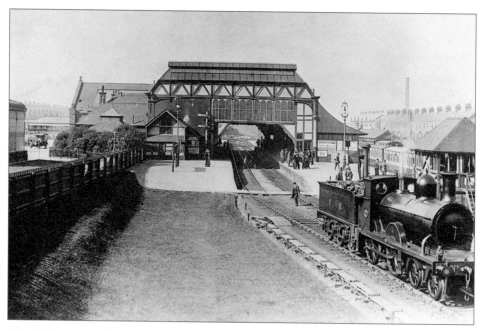

A 4–4–0 Furness Railway engine, with tender, rests outside the canopied Barrow Central station with *Copper Nob*'s glass case visible on the left, in the early twentieth century. FR carriages can be seen, right of centre; they would have been in smart blue and white livery.

Hardly recognisable as the same scene, in 2002, with even the platforms changed, we see the modern version of Barrow station. The 11.13 First North Western, Alstom-built Coreda Diesel No. 175 103, stands awaiting passengers bound for Lancaster.

Development of Barrow Shipping

A bill of sale is shown for two sixty-fourth shares in the sailing ship Lord Hartington by James Fisher, founder of the well-known shipping firm, to Richard Postlethwaite, farmer, of Rampside Hall. The ship was built in Berwick-upon-Tweed and sold in 1864. Fisher's company started in Old Barrow and then moved to Hindpool where he established the Furness Shipbuilding Company in 1870. The bill of sale was signed by father James and witnessed by son Joseph Fisher. (*See Popular History of Barrow-in-Furness by James Fisher, 1891.*)

The *Mary Sinclair* was built in 1867 at Ardrossan and was owned by Fisher's at some time. It was reputedly the 'fastest two-masted schooner sailing out of Barrow'. (*The Ashburner Schooners by Tim Latham, 1991*)

Constructed of steel, the *Result* was launched in 1893. It was said to be the 'finest small sailing vessel ever built in Britain' (Tim Latham, 1991). Some say it was once owned by Ashburner's, bought from the profits of the *Useful*.

Here we see the *Fanny Crosfield* passing Piel Island. A fine three-master, it was registered in Barrow. The ship was 95 ft 7 ins long and owned by Fisher's.

The Barrow pilot ship *Albicore*, early last century.

The *George B. Balfour* was owned by Fisher's. Of steel construction, it was launched in 1885. (*The Ashburner Schooners by Tim Latham, 1991*)

The three-masted schooner *Kelburn* seen here towed by the tug *Flying Buzzard* ran aground in Morecambe Bay in the early 1900s. The crew were reputedly taken off by Morecambe fishermen before the Fleetwood sailing lifeboat arrived. The tug was eventually broken up in Barrow.

The protected cruiser HMS *Powerful* was, at its launch in 1895, the largest ship built by Vickers in Barrow. (*Delya Slater*)

Messrs Vickers Sons and Maxim Limited launched the battleship *Vengeance* in 1899. In the Canopus class, she was fully armoured, displaced 12,950 tons and carried four 12-in and other guns, as well as four submerged torpedo tubes. (*Delya Slater*)

The paddle steamer, *Lady Evelyn*, built in 1900 for the Furness Railway Company, took passengers between Barrow and Fleetwood. In September 1914 it was renamed *Brighton Queen* and was finally sunk at Dunkirk in 1940.

On a postcard, painted in about 1904 and published by McCorquodale, we see the paddle steamer *Lady Margaret* which also sailed between Barrow and Fleetwood for the Furness Railway Company.

Two more Furness Railway Company paddle steamers, also on the Barrow to Fleetwood run, were the *Lady Moira* and the *Philomel*. This was a popular trip with passengers, often crammed cheek by jowl, seemingly overloading the boats.

Form St. 3.

Issued by the
BOARD OF TRADE
in pursuance of the
"Merchant Shipping Act, 1894."

In Duplicate. No. *2582*

PASSENGER CERTIFICATE

For a Home Trade Passenger Steam Ship,

GOING TO SEA FROM A PLACE IN THE UNITED KINGDOM ON SHORT EXCURSIONS
ALONG THE COAST DURING DAYLIGHT IN SUMMER AND IN FINE WEATHER.

To remain in force only until the *31st* day of *October*, 190*5*.

Steam Ship *Furness*

Owner, Managing Owner, or Agent *The Furness Railway Company Barrow in Furness*

Port of Registry and Official Number.	Register Tonnage.	Name of Master and Number of his Certificate.
Barrow *99943*	*15*	*Joseph Jones* *103290*

LIMITS

BEYOND WHICH THIS SHIP IS NOT TO PLY, VIZ.:—

From	To
Barrow	*Fleetwood and Blackpool*

THIS SHIP IS,

According to the declaration of the Shipwright Surveyor,

FIT TO CARRY *180* **PASSENGERS;**

WHEN THERE IS NO INCUMBRANCE OF PASSENGER ACCOMMODATION, AND SO LONG AS SHE PLIES WITHIN
THE LIMITS ABOVE STATED.

HER CREW CONSISTS OF *11* **PERSONS.**

ONE PASSENGER IS TO BE DEDUCTED FROM THE NUMBER ABOVE STATED

For every 9 square feet of Passenger accommodation occupied by Cattle, or covered by Cargo,
Luggage, or other articles.

Boats and Life-Saving Appliances.	Equipments, Distress Signals, &c.
No. *2* Life-Boats { of the aggregate capacity of } *240* Cubic feet, { and capable of accommodating } *23* Persons.	**A Fire Hose** capable of being connected with the engine, and of sufficient length to be used in any part of the vessel.
—— Boats ... { of the aggregate capacity of } —— Cubic feet, { and capable of accommodating } —— Persons.	**A Safety Valve** on each boiler, out of the control of any person on board, except the Master, when the steam is up.
—— Collapsible Boats, capable of accommodating ... ... —— Persons.	**Compasses** fixed and in good order.
—— Rafts, capable of accommodating .. .. —— Persons.	**Twelve Blue Lights.**
—— Buoyant Deck Seats, capable of supporting ... ... —— Persons.	
240 Life-Belts or other similar approved articles.	**One Cannon** and Twelve Cartridges, or other approved means of making Signals of Distress.
6 Life-Buoys.	

THIS IS TO CERTIFY that the provisions of the Law with respect to the Survey of the above-mentioned Steam
Ship, and the transmission of Declarations in respect thereof, have been complied with.

Signed by Order of the Board of Trade,

This *10th* day of *April* 190*5*

Here we see Passenger Certificate No. 2582, registered 10 April 1905, of yet another Barrow to Fleetwood boat, the *Furness*, owned by the Furness Railway Company. Its master was Joseph Jones. The maximum passenger complement was 180 or proportionally less if cattle, cargo or luggage, etc. was carried. Only two lifeboats were carried for twenty-three persons; the remaining passengers were provided with only lifebelts or six lifebuoys.

Barrow-built Holland class submarines Nos 3 and 2 are here shown with B class submarines in the background, possibly at Southampton in 1908. The Holland class were the first built at Barrow for the Royal Navy from 1901. They were not without accidents and were soon superseded by the A and B classes.

On a B&D's 'Kromo' series postcard are two Holland class submarines, this time being cleaned alongside their depot ship HMS *Hazard*, the first of its kind employed by the Royal Navy.

Royal Navy submarine C6 was launched on 20 August 1906 by Vickers Armstrongs at Barrow. It was scrapped in 1919. The similar C3 was deliberately exploded to destroy a viaduct in Zeebrugge harbour in 1918, for which the commander was awarded the Victoria Cross.

Although Royal Navy submarine L52, seen here on an early postcard, was not produced at Barrow, eighteen sister ships were launched by Vickers between 1917 and 1919. These are not to be confused with the American and Russian L class submarines.

A fine display of British sea-going craft in Buccleuch dock. From left to right we have the Isle of Man Steam Packet Company *Manxman II*, several warships, three tugs around the *Orsova* and an aircraft carrier.

A Sankey postcard shows the Vickers-built Royal Navy cruiser HMS *Cumberland* at full steam ahead. Launched in 1924 it survived the Second World War. The commanding officer in 1927 was Captain A.L. Snagge. It was the fifteenth vessel to hold this name, the first *Cumberland* being launched in 1695.

Launched in 1929, the Orient Line RMS *Orontes* was a passenger liner intended for the Australia run, but was requisitioned by the Royal Navy as a troopship during the Second World War.

The sailing lifeboat, beached near Piel.

A trio of redundant
corvettes mothballed in
Devonshire dock, *c.* 1950.
(*John Marsh*)

Royal Navy Type 42/2 destroyer HMS *Manchester* seen here at Barrow in 1982. Powered by two Rolls-Royce gas
turbines and capable of 30 knots, it was launched in the same year by Vickers.

First owned by the Furness Railway Company and registered at Barrow, the Windermere Lake steam yacht *Swift* was built in 1900 by T.B. Seath at Rutherglen. Coal was stored in an enclosure that is now part of the Lakeside car park and loaded in skips. The yacht was later converted to diesel. (*Raphael Tuck card for the Furness Railway Company*)

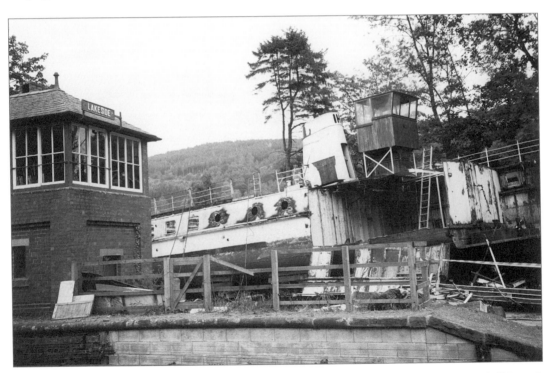

Recently the *Swift*, at the end of its service life, was berthed at Lakeside, used for a time for the 'Campbell Legend Exhibition' and finally broken for scrap, as seen here in 1998.

In Devonshire dock with the Devonshire Dock Hall behind is the Royal Navy SSBN nuclear-powered submarine HMS *Vanguard*. Launched in 1992, it carries Trident missiles.

Auxiliary oiler RFA *Wave Knight*, here being fitted out in Buccleuch dock, was launched by BAE Systems at Barrow in 2001. Its sister ship, *Wave Ruler*, was built by BAE Systems at Govan. (*John Marsh*)

Buccleuch dock, 2002. On the left is the P&O vessel *European Mariner*. Opposite are twin LPDs (landing platform docks), assault ships HMS *Albion* and HMS *Bulwark*, intended to transport troops, landing craft and helicopters.

In 2002, inconspicuous in Devonshire dock, left of centre we have HMS *Ursula*, one of four Royal Navy conventional diesel-electric-powered Upholder class submarines, being converted for the Canadian Navy by BAE Systems. All are renamed: *Upholder, Unseen, Ursula* and *Unicorn* became or will become *Chicoutimi, Victoria, Corner Brook* and *Windsor*.

Dalton & Low Furness Villages

A photograph by Hargreaves of Dalton, in the 1914 Barrow and District Year Book, is of the maypole dance performed at Dalton on May Day 1913 for an attentive crowd. On the same day 'Miss Nina Dixon was enthroned as Queen of the Revels'.

The old Roa Island lifeboat station as it was in June 1999. Roa Island is linked to the mainland by a road causeway, once carrying a Furness Railway line. Before this the surrounding harbour was known as Pile-a-Foudre, being first surveyed extensively by Lieutenant Thomas Evans RN in about 1829.

The same scene in April 2001 shows the new lifeboat station with refurbished approach and new slipway. Piel Island and castle are to the right. A sketch of Piel, Foulney and Roa islands, spelt Peele, Fouley and Roe, was sent to Samuel Pepys, the diarist, in 1667 when he was Secretary to the Admiralty. (*John Marsh*)

A view from an elevated point in about 1900 captures the Furness Railway train at Roa Island terminus. The railway line along the relatively wide causeway can be seen disappearing towards Rampside. (*Moira Ness*)

In this photograph, taken from raised ground in 2002, the site of the old railway terminus has been covered but the end of the road causeway is seen with some of the buildings still present on the right. Vessels from the Roa Island Boating Club are visible on the left.

Rampside Hall, 1905. Its curious set of twelve square chimneys is known as the Twelve Apostles. The frontage shows five windows with the wall surface almost completely covered in creeper. The hall was occupied by the Knipe family at some time in the sixteenth and seventeenth centuries.

In 2002 the hall has been restored to having fourteen front windows – as in its original design. Modern housing is evident on the left.

The Clarke's Arms hotel, Rampside, early last century, photographed by J. Atherton of Barrow.

In 2002, smartly decorated, having lost a door but gained a front porch, renamed the Clarke's hotel and brasserie and with a neat car park, it advertises 'Non residents welcome. All rooms ensuite. Executive standard. Try our special weekend breaks. Notice the difference.' Note the same sturdy tree on the right.

Two views, the first by Sankey, of the same stretch of the Coast Road separated by around 100 years. At Newbiggin Bay an unperturbed motorist in the middle of the road is replaced by one obeying hazard lines in 2002.

The Coast Road continues to the Point of Comfort with Goadsbarrow bay on the left. The upper postcard is by Sankey. In the lower picture the grass has grown somewhat in nearly 100 years.

Postmarked 1930, this Sankey postcard shows Baycliffe in the parish of Aldingham and variously, from the thirteenth to the fifteenth century, known as Belleclive, Beleclyve, Belclyf or Beelclyf. It is situated on the Coast Road, halfway between Ulverston and Barrow, near to the Morecambe Bay shoreline.

By 2002 the village is much enlarged. At the bend in the road on the right is the Fisherman's Arms.

A historic village, Urswick, has traces of neolithic settlement in its limestone and a church with a thirteenth-century tower. Here, part of Great Urswick is seen from Clark Beck on the other side of Urswick tarn. The legend of the tarn is worth a read. (See J.P. Morris, *The North Lonsdale Magazine* and *Lake District Miscellany* p. 90, 1866.)

From a point close to Clark Beck we have a wider view of the village. The tarn supports numerous waterfowl including waterhen, coot, geese and mallard.

Market Street, Dalton-in-Furness, on a Sankey postcard delivered in 1931. Dalton was described in 1829 as 'rising to provincial eminence under the fostering hand of King Stephen. It consists of one good street terminated by a spacious market place, where an old castle, consisting of a square tower, overlooks the town, and gives it an air of dignity.' The old Roxy cinema shows as the white building right of centre.

Apart from the demise of the Roxy, there has been little change to the buildings by 2002. The gaslight has been moved away from the tightly disciplined parking spaces and is replaced by a neat tentative lamp peering over the cars. All the A590 traffic used to pass this way but a welcome bypass has now been provided.

In the early 1900s Askam village was provided with a flourishing iron works (centre) and brick works (left foreground). The River Duddon is beyond with Black Combe overlooking. A wisp of smoke can just be seen below Black Combe summit – the Millom iron works. The only feature marking the Askam name on the 1847, 6 in. Ordnance Survey map is a wood. (*Delya Slater*)

Both Millom and Askam iron works have disappeared by 2002 but the brick works still flourishes. It still has roughly the same layout but has lost its smaller chimney.

Eton collars signify early last century for this picture of Duke Street, the main shopping area of Askam. The iron works is nearby with the aptly named Vulcan hotel on the left. Iron ore was everywhere. The iron mines at Roanhead were only a mile away.

The same scene at Askam in 2002 is much changed left of centre. The iron works is replaced by housing. The Vulcan hotel buildings have been been upgraded. Travel down the nearby Duddon Road to Duddon sands and you have an excellent beach walk north to Dunnerholme rock and golf links.

Sankey photographed Askam, with the older Ireleth village and the moors beyond, from the top of an iron works' slag bank, *c.* 1910.

In 2002, viewed from the top of the same slag bank which is now overgrown, Askam is much changed. The line of buildings, from the row of terraced houses in Sharp Street via a gable end to the building with a chamfered corner, the Furness Tavern, still exists. Market Street is obscured by stylish new housing.

A fine limestone building, the Council schools in Askam, outside the village, *c.* 1910. The headmistress in 1940 was Miss Birch, who was accompanied by Miss Crawford and Mrs Shaw.

A more oblique view of the school in 2002 shows the lengthened front windows. The roadside wall has been replaced by railings and the school renamed Askam Village Foundation School.

Douglas's Old King's Head in Church Street, Broughton in Furness, *c.* 1900, caught by S.M. Gibson & Co. of Gateshead-on-Tyne. It has what may be a collection of water pumps on the left.

The decoration has totally changed and now, in 2002, the hotel is simply named the Old King's Head. The sash windows remain with an extra one replacing the left-hand door, and the house to the right has gained a storey.

The atmosphere of Stainton quarry limestone crusher plant is well represented here as painted by artist Allan Smith of Rampside.

Viewed from a similar point in 2002, the plant has been replaced by the large mound in the centre of the photograph. Limestone is still exported from the quarry. Reputedly having a high calcium content, it is used in the manufacture of calcium carbide.

A 1909 postcard depicts the old sea mill, a rarity in Furness, near the shore at Bardsea. Power was provided by sea water filling and emptying the mill pond via a channel from the tide.

The mill in 2002 is now gone and the pond ornamental, graced by swans and waterfowl. The Old Mill café nearby serves a good variety of wholesome food.

The approach to Bardsea village was caught on this postcard, *c.* 1910. From the muddy sands of Morecambe Bay the entrance/exit channel bridge and drain for the sea mill water supply can be seen left of centre. The two boats on the foreshore would be an unusual sight today.

From a viewpoint closer to the drain in 2002 we again see Bardsea Holy Trinity church on the right, itself having a commanding view of Morecambe Bay. The church was consecrated in 1853. On the left are a few extra buildings at the foot of the hill.

Inside Bardsea village, shown on this Raphael Tuck postcard sent in 1905, was Bardsea Hall. It had eighteen bedrooms and a schoolroom. Once the seat of the Bardsey family, it was described as an 'Ancient Mansion House' when it was sold in 1918. An extensive demolition sale was held in 1927.

In 2002 all that remains of the hall is the front gate, on the left of the picture, facing the main road through the village.

Well House, Bardsea, on a postcard of about 1910 and photographed by J. Thompson of Blake Street, Barrow. It was built in about 1640 and faces, although is obscured from, Morecambe Bay. It lies down a quiet narrow lane close to Bardsea Green.

The house is now a Grade II listed building and still stands in 2002, although now hidden by a different collection of trees. Note the circular chimney on the right.

At the first crossroads on the way out of Bardsea towards Ulverston stood this lodge. Photographed by S.S. Crewdson of Ulverston, *c.* 1880, it was close to Little Head Wood and Conishead Priory. The building was completely redesigned in 1885 as seen in the picture below.

In 2002 the lodge with Conishead Priory, now the Manjushri Buddhist Centre, in the background, stands at an entrance to Oxley Developments Company Limited.

An early high-winged monoplane was photographed in about 1910 with Hoad monument in the background and with an orderly crowd more interested in the camera than the plane. The aircraft carried trippers for short flights from a 'flying ground at Mountbarrow'.

In the 1920s, probably from the same airstrip, 'Captain C.S. Kent, the intrepid airman, gave exhibitions of flying skill, his daring evolutions thrilling large numbers of spectators'.

Ulverston

Glaxo baby food, sold by Joseph Nathan & Co. Ltd, was burlesqued early last century on this postcard photographed by J. Wilkinson of Wigton. The sign was prophetic in that Ulverston has literally fed on Glaxo, now GlaxoSmithKline, which has provided employment since the factory was opened in 1948.

This 1905 postcard shows Princes Street, Ulverston, with Thomas Briggs Limited, drapers, almost opposite to MacDonald's temperance hotel which was at the start of Queen Street at the corner of Cavendish Street. The Market Place is just visible in the distance.

In 2002 the temperance hotel is the GlaxoSmithKline Sports and Social Club, more visible because many of the old buildings were removed when the A590 road was cut through the town in about 1966.

A dejected Market Place, Ulverston, is shown on this photograph from the H. Kitchen series of postcards, *c.* 1850. The Phoenix Fire Office is on the right. Blurred images of figures in the centre witness the long exposure times necessary in those days. Other traders in the square included T.T. Briggs, check manufacturer, Robert Bell, chair maker and Peters & Lister, iron founders. The old fishstones enclose the island in the centre.

In 2002, with a one-way traffic system, the marketplace retains most of its old buildings except for those replaced by the Westminster bank left of centre. An open market, under a charter since the reign of Edward I, is still held here on Thursdays. The fish slabs have been replaced by the cenotaph.

A 'Sankey high speed photograph' on an early postcard shows the middle of Market Street with the square beyond, *c.* 1910. Stainton & Wignall, drapers, E. & M. Garnett, fruiterers and Marsden's butchers are on the left with the Farmer's Arms, G.H. Mackereth's, Hume Kitchen's, booksellers (?), and G. Moralee's, drapers, in the distance.

In 2002 the much-debated cobblestones are still in place, the pavement is modified, the buildings are intact, the old grey town has been decorated and the street is now one-way for motorists.

At the bottom end of Market Street, *c.* 1933. Armstrong Siddeley F 3657, the Ulverston police motor patrol car, has just been serviced at Arthur Jones's garage. Note the narrow tyres. Sergeant Huxley and Constable Kidd are seated, ready to drive away. (*B.V. Jones*)

At 3 p.m. by the Savings Bank clock in April 2002 we see Market Street as a congested one-way system with little or no change in the buildings.

On the left an Ulverston Hospitals Saturday Parade notice advertises a Saturday May Day carnival with May queen and ten brass bands in the first decade of the last century. Here we see a parade in New Market Street, with choristers in (possibly red) cassocks and mortarboards and white surplices from Holy Trinity church, followed by three tuba players leading a band.

One-way New Market Street in 2002 is lined with cars. On the extreme right Images has replaced the Victorian part of the Sun hotel. The market hall and shops on the left, beyond, are where the old market house was before its disastrous fire.

Birketts County Drapery Stores at the end of New Market Street and on County Square is seen on a James Atkinson postcard, *c.* 1919. The Birkett family included Lord Birkett of Ulverston, who was one of the British judges at the Nuremburg trial and Lord Justice of Appeal from 1950 to his retirement in 1957.

In 2002 the shop frontage has been modified and a number of chimneys removed. On the left F.J. Harrison's county auction rooms are now occupied by Harrison & Coward, valuers, estate agents and auctioneers.

On the other side of County Square in about 1900 the building on the right was occupied by the London City & Midland Bank Company Limited. Opposite this in 1907 on Cavendish Street corner was the Bank of Liverpool, the manager of which was W.A. Antliff. The postcard is by Valentine's.

The handsome building on the left, with its characteristic green dome, is now, in 2002, occupied by Barclays Bank plc. The building right of centre was, for a time, the county library but this is now in a modern building in Kings Road.

At the corner of Lightburn Road and Victoria Road, as seen on this 1913 postcard by James Atkinson, were the Roman Catholic church, dedicated to St Mary of Furness, and presbytery. The church's foundation stone was laid in 1893. In 1929 the presbytery was occupied by Fathers J. and Oliver E. Morrissy.

By 2002 the church buildings externally have changed little, the presbytery roof having lost its dormer window. A lych-gate has appeared and the tree on the corner has been removed. Although the tree near the church door has thickened considerably it has not been allowed to increase in height.

A group of teachers from Lightburn School, *c.* 1930. Back row, left to right: Arthur Athersmith, Percy Hibbert, Edward Winstone, -?-; middle row: Edwin Roberts, -?-, -?-, Annie Jones, -?-; in front: Will Tyson.

The school, erected in 1914, is now, in 2002, named the Sir John Barrow School. On the right is Argyll Street with the house where the comedian Stan Laurel was born in 1890. A plaque outside the front door commemorates the event.

This card by James Atkinson, posted in 1907, shows St Mary's parish church and Hart Street's Victoria Grammar School, which was opened in 1900. The school was built to replace the old Town Bank Grammar School, then 250 years old. The church is part Norman.

In 2002 we see the once handsome front of the school boarded up. Its fate is in the balance. The school was no longer needed when the classes moved to Springfield Road. The rubble on the field is the remains of the more modern school extension, which was only recently used as a hostel for refugees from Kosovo.

Seen on a Frith's postcard, Ulverston Park in 1929 supported two concrete and four red shale tennis courts, two bowling greens, a putting green, a set of swings and a see-saw. The facilities were well used. Left of centre are the tennis changing room, toilets and garden tool shed, with the park keeper's hut on its left.

In 2002 the park shows the two bowling greens neglected – a flower bed is in the middle of the one on the right. The park is little used but fortunately the grass and flower beds are still kept in order.

Acknowledgements

My thanks are due to: Thomas and Ruth Bircher, Tom Dawson, Andrew Hanson with British Gas Hydrocarbon Resources Ltd, Brian V. Jones, M.H.R. Kennedy, Tim Latham, John Marsh, Moira Ness, Delya Slater, Allan Smith, Mike Smith with BAE Systems, Denis and Margaret Stanswood, the Vicar and Verger of St George's church, Barrow, and the manager of the NatWest offices in Ramsden Square, Barrow, variously, for permission to take or use photographs and for helpful guidance; also to the many people I met in photographing Barrow. All were enthusiastic and encouraging in relating the history and changes which have taken place in the town. I am also indebted to the early photographers without whose contribution this book could not have been compiled.

Every effort has been made to trace the owners of copyright of pictures or text used in the book. All pictures without a credit belong to the author.